BLISS PIG
and other poems

BLISS PIG
and other poems

**LINDA STITT
CHARLENE JONES**

Natural Heritage / Natural History Inc.

Copyright © 1999 by Linda Stitt and Charlene Jones
All rights reserved. No portion of this book, with the exception of brief extracts for the purpose of literary or scholarly review, may be reproduced in any form without the permission of the publisher.

Published by Natural Heritage/Natural History Inc.
P.O. Box 95, Station O, Toronto, Ontario M4A 2M8

Design by Norton Hamill Design
Edited by Jane Gibson
Printed and bound in Canada by Hignell Printing Limited

Canadian Cataloguing in Publication Data

Jones, Charlene, 1952 -
    Bliss pig and other poems

ISBN 1-896219-60-8

I. Stitt, Linda, 1932 -   . II. Title.

PS8569.O495B54 1999   C811'.54   C99-931738-5
PR9199.3.J66B54 1999

The Canada Council | Le Conseil des Arts
for the arts | du Canada
since 1957 | depuis 1957

Natural Heritage/Natural History Inc. acknowledges the support received for its publishing program from the Canada Council Block Grant Program. We also acknowledge with gratitude the assistance of the Association for the Export of Canadian Books, Ottawa.

DEDICATION

To Cecilie
the other third member of Uncritical Mass who has
graciously permitted us to include her poem

Lacking constancy, I write
on rivers, the words and letters
swirl around a bend
eddy into hopeless tangles
of inchoherency. Tree tops, then.
The smooth trunk of arbutus
pushes papery bark to forest floor;
lear litter and alpha beta indecipherable
from the rainbow scrawl of slug.
Grappling with wisps of cloud
I form them into symbol,
picture of intent, desire,
but they trail away in higher flows
become muddied by the smoke
of spring cleaning fires.
All this while my mind moves
toward the ghost of who you might have been
(and who was I, then?) The scent
of our connection pungent, strong, yet
when I try to land it, bring it in,
the words swoop toward me, then drop
rise, scatter into this landscape;
dissolve, become inseparably part
of what, in leaving, I have left undone.

CECILIE

ACKNOWLEDGMENTS

We would like to express our immoderate thanks to our publishers and editors, Barry, Jane and Nancy Penhale and Heather Wakeling. We are grateful for their support, the expertise and their faith.

LINDA STITT and CHARLENE JONES
(two-thirds of Uncritical Mass)

HOMAGE TO CANADA COUNCIL

Two poets of small recognition
were losing their spark and ambition
till a government grant
made Can out of can't
and now they're hell bent for perdition.

LINDA STITT

FOLK POETRY

Academics we are not;
our written work is never fraught.
We don't pretend to erudition;
folk poetry is our ambition.

CHARLENE JONES and LINDA STITT

CONTENTS

Acknowledgements 7

LINDA STITT
    Homage to Canada Council 9
    Folk Poetry 9
    Apologia 13
    Sense of Purpose 15
    Transported 25
    Time Out 26
    Charity Begins 29
    Crone 35
    Linda's Lament 39
    Refuge 42
    Advice to Women 46
    Body Wisdom 47
    Long Range Romance 49
    Bliss Pig 52
    Come As You Are
      or Beauty Of The Beast 55
    How Was It For You Baby? 56
    Crying Shame 60
    Love Poem 63
    Prison Ship 66
    For Peter—Ciao 67
    Regrets 72
    In Extremis 75
    Discrimination Aspiration 77
    In The Bone 78
    Heritage 79
    Daughter's Poem 80
    Past Due 86
    Death Wish 91
    Depth Recollection 92
    Void Essence 93

Spindrift 94
Old Age Security 95
Off Duty But In Service 96
Music Teacher 98
Polishing My Footwork 99
Born Again…And Again… 100
Vehicle Inspection 101
Approaching My 67th Birthday 102

CHARLENE JONES
Folk Poetry 9
Writer's Instructions 14
My God 17
Dear God: 19
Three Kinds of Gods 21
Rainbows 23
Lilith Fair and Square 27
Feast or Famine 30
Light Plays 32
NightSky Woman 33
mother/earth 37
Story 44
Love 48
Useful Boys 51
Pig Dreams 53
The Man In Black 54
And If You Don't Call 57
Fast Love 58
The Tenth Mountain 61
Kiss 62
Midnight Woman 64
My Son 68
Leave Taking 69
go stupid 70
The Line I Forgot 74
Rosemary 82
My Mother 84
Old Gods 88
When I Go Out Of Here 89

APOLOGIA

If in some poems we neglect

          TO BE POLITICALLY
             CORRECT

we beg your patience

          AND YOUR KIND
             INDULGENCE.

Discretion,

          THOUGH WE TRULY TRY,

on most occasions leaves us shy

          OF ITS COMPLETE AND
             UNABRIDGED EFFULGENCE.

We may

          WHEN OPPORTUNITY ALLOWS,

milk humour out of sacred cows

          OR ROLL AWAY THE STONE
             WHERE AXES GRIND.

Solemnity appears to us

          WHEN MUCH INDULGED

ridiculous

          AND FOSTERS FARCE IN
          OUR COLLECTIVE MIND.

We don't mean to offend one's pride

          OR TO BELITTLE OR DERIDE

but assholes have a tendency
   to tighten up,

          SO PLEASE

forgive the odd rash word,

          WE'RE LUDICROUS

but life's absurd.

          LET'S LOOSEN UP

and live it up

          AND LIGHTEN UP.

LINDA STITT

WRITER'S INSTRUCTIONS

The first rule of thumb in writing is to avoid using clichés. The reason for this as every Tom, Dick and Harry agree, is there's no use flogging a dead horse. Even though you can't put old heads on young shoulders some beginning writers believe in using what's tried and true; as a result they end up between the devil and the deep blue sea, neither fish nor land, between a rock and a hard place. What they miss is that communication of meaning relies on the real McCoy and requires sometimes the patience of Job. Further, although great minds do think alike, it is easy to be caught titling at windmills, when the true experience involves putting your shoulder to the grindstone. That way you follow the advice as old as Methuselah: avoid clichés!

CHARLENE JONES

SENSE OF PURPOSE

What can I offer to totality,
      the source of all made manifest?
What can I give in gratitude
for this extraordinary life

Only to act as mirror to the all,
  reflecting self to self,
    another facet
      on the infinite jewel of creation.

Look, I say,
I give you the uniqueness of experience
of this infinitesimal cell
of your eternal being.

Here is the smell of roses
to this particular nose
and this is the stench of diesel fumes.
This is the slide of silk along this skin,
the touch of the fingertip to lip.
Here is how the breath feels,
breathing in,
trickling, flowing, rushing out.
This is the act of chewing, tasting,
    bitter, salty sour and sweet.
And this is walking,
watching how the feet
are lifting, moving, placing,
on concrete, carpet, grass.

This is the celebration of the intellect,
the joyous leap of intuition.
Here is the issue of your root
growing to limitless fruition.

This is the swirl of love,
the rush of fear,
the body's fireworks serpent of sensation.

This is devotion.
This is adoration.

The full awareness of the senses
and of mind
I strive to offer you in every moment,
to feed into the universal consciousness
this aspect, this view,
this yet another flavour of perception,
this blissful expression of participation,
    like a child's drawing
        to be hung on God's refrigerator door.

LINDA STITT

MY GOD

I look for god in Harvey's in Wal-mart,
walk through downtown streets
where cars screech and horns beep
and rumbles of noise from blocks away
sound under the skyscrapers
I'm craning my head to see,
bring me closer, draw me nearer
to my god.

My god wears thin denim jeans
from the bargain basement
my god gobbles fast food
and sometimes, my god stands
under a tree with me
watching the sparrows
and muttering through his spittle

my god a neon sign
banging itself in the wind

my god curls into pool halls
like cigarette smoke,
my god drinks gin

my god smiles a toothless grin
in the atery city dawn
of October when there's no shelter
and the hand-outs are all gone

My god pulls the blanket closer
gathers the children for night on the street
my god is the one with dirty hair
who talks to herself and can't sleep

this god staggers homeward
to find the house gone
my god then turns barefeet west
and just walks on and on.

CHARLENE JONES

DEAR GOD:

I remember praying to you and your son every night since I was little. I remember looking for you at communion service, rolling my eyes past the piled-high collection plate, its brass colour turning to gold in the sun streaming from the stained glass windows which I looked out to find you, and didn't. I looked in the back pews of the church with that choir boy, 'till the priest threw us both out, and I still didn't find you. I kept looking. At the university, the coffee shop, the corner drugstore even out the trucking route to the nearest port city. I looked in an ocean freighter hoping to find you and found a job instead sailing to England where I still didn't find you but bumped into some people who said you could be found in psychedelics and opiates so crossing over the mid-east into Afghanistan in those pre-Soviet invasion days I tried to find you in the drugs and placebos and several times called your name but I did not find you. And trekking on to Tibet in Tibetan monasteries where it was said you lived in the breath of man and could be found by dialing a mantra over and over I mantra'd till my breath froze in that frigid air while I gazed unwaveringly at the solid gold Buddha statue and wondered where you were. Abandoning the Dial-A-God attempt, I hiked through the New Zealand mountains in search of sacred Maori burial grounds, where the ancients were said to be interred in caskets inlaid with precious gems and so suffering the chill of night, the heat of day, it was for you I searched. And even in those towns of Melbourne, Sydney, Christchurch, Welland, posting those notices for like-minded people and starting that commune with those seven heirs who eventually threw me out because I could not help them find you, it was for you I sought. And back here again on the west coast in one bar and another and another actualizing my impatience with life myself and everything until I stumbled on the power of visualization and positive affirmations through which I have learned to participate in shaping the direction of my life by contracting the part of me which is you so here it is:

I want to be rich. Not rich on a relative scale. Not rich compared to medieval kings who despite moats and castles had no toilets. Not rich compared to Most People. I mean stinking, filthy rich. I mean piles mounds of green bills worth $1,000.00; I mean enough of them to sole the sandals I wear only once. Enough so I can buy a new yacht whenever the liquor cabinet is empty. I mean that rich. And I don't mean opening my eyes to daily riches, sparrows and lilies and all that. Not the King Midas stuff either: my health or happiness or those I love for the dough I want it all, my health, happiness, those I love *and* the money. I want this because all my searches have taught me the scriptures were right: you live in a mansion.

Dedicated to wealth in your name,
I remain faithfully yours

CHARLENE JONES

THREE KINDS OF GODS

Three kinds of gods argue through my life
as though it were a thing of beauty, gossamer, and unchal-
lenged
by the weight of material.
These gods insist, each in their way,
for propitiation in the same moment
and so I am bowing and scraping to the east
offering bowls of water on my knees
and all the while eager for that thrust between my legs
the mounting of Pan.

Three kinds of gods impart a modicum
of what might pass as insight
on a day impaled by pollution,
The slice of knowledge
covered in its own sweat, shivers,
eager for a coat of any colour.
This is Hermes, also Manjusuri, Quetzacoatle
Joseph and possibly the Black Madonna
          (although when she dances
you easily lose sight in her magnificent spray of rage)
and if it's Tuesday, join these with a saint or two
beatified by those in High Office.

I'm not sure yet of the significance in all directions
the sudden shadows upon my wall
or why the chanting rings across that plain over there
the one below us now
rings like a holy brass bowl and bong
that echoes like a sway of iris.

I'm certain but catch suddenly in the grip of my toes
that flush from the secret center
        dark scent like earth
        of moss, of fragrant, moist flowers
                      and mold
        that rush with its hallelujah chorus
                welcome to the thrust of life

    that one,
        makes me weep, bend down
                      make offerings.

CHARLENE JONES

RAINBOWS

When a rainbow walks the sun splatters colour and camels, cacti, crystals leap and dangle or grow between the bands of light, music calypso, mamba, reggae, rock harmonic in off-key syncopated swing with hips and someone said Debbie is the one who taught me to dance.

If a rainbow ranges from one rock wide across the sky to another rock garden or pot of gold, you stand akimbo, amazed, alert to a sudden flash like indigo birds or antique caravans, a taste like fresh mangoes and melted chocolate, although her kitchen has no pots, few plates and no tea towels, her fridge is a place to store paint and furniture stripper, her cupboards are stripped and hold long stemmed wine glasses and the coffee does not quit until the rainbow zings inside your eyes, too.

Longing for a rainbow makes no never mind, rainbows fade or bless according to whim and mysterious gravitational effects of the earth's tilt, of wind systems and, of course, solar dust storms. Rainbows know this can't quite be said, they just up and leave and back again when the time is right. Try to touch a rainbow and it sheds itself before you, colours fading and splaying into the wider sky. Push too hard, a rainbow's sudden thunder rages its underside and there you stand, under dark, angry clouds and the rain part.

Then in a taxicab a sudden three hour conversation leads to years of friendship because the rainbow had returned and no one else can listen or hear with the intensity of blue light, like a rainbow.

Should a rainbow open, the smallest dream slides through hoops as easily as cat's cradle or the delicate shifting of shape on her daughter's face, the one face Rainbow can't refuse.

For everyone else, it's business as usual, a slide on magic carpets going to blues clubs, a sudden turned up look at bright, fiery stars glowing across Boston where, someone said, Debbie was the only one to get me to skinny dip in a hot pool.

The only one. The rainbow you're seeing feels like the only one you've ever seen, and is, and in a world like this, rainbows are few and far between. Thank you rainbow for being and for having been.

CHARLENE JONES

TRANSPORTED

More and more
I am captured by beauty.

It seizes me
in filigreed fronds
sprouting through the mottled bark
of an ailanthus tree,
    draws me
    with the magnetic green
    of a mallard's magnificence,
    ambushes me
    in a lily of the valley's
    cupped fragrance,
        waylays me
        with shimmering showers
        flung by a bathing sparrow.

Wherever I walk,
contemplating the ache of impermanence,
beauty lies in wait
to seduce me with poignancy
from the pain of flesh.

                LINDA STITT

TIME OUT

We were always One.
There was only One;
there never was
anyone else.

But just to make the sport more scary
we played at the game of adversary
and hid ourselves in mysteries
swathed in our separate histories
and dreamed of finding One.

But it was always One.
One hung upon the cross,
One sat beneath the bodhi tree,
and One was good,
and One was bad,
and One was all there'll ever be,
      shaman and cynic, sinner and saint.

Behind the mask,
beneath the paint,
beyond the blade of arbitrary time,
there has been One,
      integral and sublime,
being whatever, however, whoever it chose to be,
      being you,
      being me,
           being itself in myriad manifestation.

And, not to spoil the game,
but just to have a moment's celebration,
let's recollect with love and jubilation,
that we are One.

                                      LINDA STITT

LILITH FAIR AND SQUARE

I am Lilith, 1st wife of Adam—
you don't hear much about me.
Your Yawheh/Jehovah called me up
said, "I've got a favour to ask, you wanna get married?"

I laughed, "Oh, God after all this time
you and I been friends,
making oceans, gardens, mountains,
playing at creation, now you want..."

"No, it's Adam."

I did pause. This required some thought.
1st Lady of The Garden...not bad, not bad.

I married him because God was on the spot—
a whole world to populate
and no one with whom Adam could copulate.

So, as a favour mind you, to an old friend
I offered what I believe to be the richest gift you can conceive...
my body, this flesh, the earth, blessed earth.
But Adam could not see my worth.

She won't lie beneath me, he whined to God.
She wants to be on top half the time.

God tried. He said, "Couldn't you accommodate her,
son of mine?"

Adam said, "But she's pigheaded, adventurous, creative,
opinionated, daring, outspoken, enthusiastic,
competitive, and well, God

for a girl, she's extremely odd."
God said to me, "Now look, the kid's upset.
He's new to this life and well
he wants a different kind of wife.
What say you go outside the garden
go adventuring, call it a fling
and finish naming everything."

He knew I'd do this anyway. You see, where he
wanted to be the One God, that's why he invented
Adam, I know real life thrusts in all life -
I know he doesn't have as much control
as, for a SkyGod, he thinks he should.
I know the thousand names of God right here
right now on this earth in its beauty
and if I wanted to, I could...

But, o well. It didn't look so good
being 1st Lady of The Garden after all.
Not if I had to beg for affection and respect.
I'd rather be out on what you might call
the dark side of the moon
dancing on the thin line of the equator at noon.

That's where you'll see me still
juggling all of creation
and calling it by its real name—God!
God Roses! God Rainbows! God Drought!
God Rivers and Waters! God Sunshine! God Grass!
God...well, you get the picture.

Everything is God. I know that. That's why
when I hear the press he gets,
how God Created Everything. I just smile,
I know Everything Created God.

CHARLENE JONES

CHARITY BEGINS

The impulse
  to give
    transcends thought.

Deeper than duty,
  more innate than intention,
    it inhabits the heart.

Where dana dwells,
three jewels manifest
  and emptiness
  holds nothing back
  from emptiness.

Nothing is diminished
as the winds blow
and grow still.

Potential
blossoms into myriad forms,
  not to be grasped
  or hoarded.

Giving
is the spirit's wisdom
and compassion,
  refusing to accept
  the fallacy
  of giver and receiver,
    seeing only the flux and flow
    of infinity at play.

LINDA STITT

FEAST OR FAMINE

In Somalia, picture says, a little girl
holds the stick figure of her brother,
who will die soon. She will bury him.

I cut a tomatoe, slice through the center
        my son has gone to a friend's house to play...

the rug needs cleaning, but not this month
I am going to pay the chimney sweep...

in Somalia, it was Cambodia, it was Bangladesh
I was sixteen crying to my father

the radio playing
I'm a soul man
good lovin' I got a truckload

of food can't get through, rifles
bayonetters, the last of their money
gone to supply weapons while

my soul is the earth, my heart
and here are some of mine, starving...

I turn the bacon, rinds of fat
of the land, while 1,500 humans died
of starvation...

God grant me the serenity to accept

a god whose position has to do
with warring tribal factions
thousands of years ago
whose legacy to me now is

Somalians will die by the hundreds
of thousands in Ethiopia and Kenya
the children of Nicaragua, Brazil

reading the fall catalogue
shopping for new selections
I can't seem to find the right
colour and size.

CHARLENE JONES

LIGHT PLAYS

The way light plays
t.v. screen contains
the colour of flowers
blooming across the room
and, o, a cactus
in the maple tree outside
front double windows
cactus lives behind glass
on my inside stairwell.
This riot, profusion, tangram
confusion
comforts me,
who cannot see
the line clearly between
which me is me.

CHARLENE JONES

NIGHTSKY WOMAN

A beautiful woman lives in the sky
and holds her breath all day
but when the sky begins to darken
she comes out to play.

She opens her lovely mouth
and breathes out all the stars.
She makes a sigh and all the winds
go blowing near and far.

She takes the colour from the flowers
and leaves off every tree.
She puts the colours in her pockets
neatly as can be.

She tucks in all the goats and sheep
the cows and horses too.
She pats each one, sings them to sleep
with a soft hullaloo, hullaloo.

She wanders by the rivers
besides the lakes and ponds
she gathers all the dancing light
from each and every one.

She plucks the sunlight from each wave
all the dancing sparks
she piles them in a bucket
so the waters grow quite dark.

The beautiful woman then sits very still
and breathes softly out and in
and all night long her breathing weaves
the darkness we all sleep in.

Then as the sun begins to rise
she sighs one big long sigh
then rises holds her breath
and vanishes against the sky.

CHARLENE JONES

CRONE

I have experienced babe through infant,
adolescent, maiden, mother
matriarch and crone.
I have seen a lot of change,
wondrous and strange
and I have learned to live alone.

I have learned a lot of things,
forgotten many,
especially names,
   —sometimes my own.
But that's okay,
it demonstrates
just one more aspect of impermanence.
>   Mental acuity
>   is not granted
>   in perpetuity.

And the me I guard so jealously
is not the only Pisces in the sea.

I am a fleeting flower
in the garden of the boundless,
a momentary manifestation
and I declare my cronehood
the age of celebration.
Now I can call all young men Sonny
and threaten cyclists on the sidewalk with my cane
and speak my mind in service of the one mind,
simple and plain
and infinitely complex.
>   I know the world just has to hear
>   what I just have to say.
>   If not,

it doesn't matter anyway,
I'm gone tomorrow,
here today,
simply a brief out picturing
of the universe at play.

And, playing crone,
I learn myself
in endless variation
and teach totality
a life
of its compassionate creation.

LINDA STITT

mother/earth

I dream with you
               I dream with you
your milky mouth at my milk laden breast
I dream your body
               dream your body
Break me open
radiant   scattered
your suckling lips
teach my nipples to exist
seasons erupt from my breasts
ripe fruit   fresh snow

Your body sings
               itself into form
shaping new each morning
your body climbed from my dream
when you were born

Break me open
pagan   savage
your bite etches
the bruise of autumn
ripe fruit dripping from my mouth

O Web Child! Star Child!
I dream you, I dream you!

And dream with you
               now you move through space
unbound from the constant need of my face.

Break me open
your heart   my earth
love spins us on our axis

I dream with you
          the nights of our sleep
and dreaming wake, and waking weep
the joy of life unweaves in you, too.

I dream with you,
          I dream with you.

CHARLENE JONES

LINDA'S LAMENT

I think I know what's happening,
why everything's less than fine.
I'm caught in someone else's karma.
It certainly can't me mine.

Somebody else's karma,
flung from I don't know where,
like a well chewed wad of bubble gum
has landed in my hair.

I know I lead a blameless life,
I know I'm worth my salt,
I know that the crap that's coming at me
is definitely not my fault.

I've cut right back on hatred and greed
and the succulent sins of the flesh
and the bread I cast on the waters
is reasonably clean and fresh.

I'm the soul of generosity,
patient and sweet and kind,
so all you gods who have obviously goofed,
please fix things, if you wouldn't mind.

They say that everything comes around,
but to me it's perfectly clear
that whatever came and clobbered me from behind
sure didn't start out here.

I won't get into specifics,
its like having your computer fail
or getting trapped in an elevator
or breaking a fingernail.

There are troubles large and troubles small
to which I'm sure you can relate,
like growing a fluorescent zit on your nose
just before an important date.

Or catching your dearest gentleman friend
in your garter belt and wig,
or developing laryngitis the day
of a very prestigious gig.

It's like losing your wallet and credit cards,
like losing your faith and your nerve,
like losing face and getting it back
with wrinkles you don't deserve.

It's a crime, it's a crock, it's a dirty shame,
it's a downright bloody disgrace;
somebody who had it coming ducked
and I got the pie in the face.

It's like stepping in a pile of dog shit.
It happens so very quick,
it seeps into the crevices of your shoes
and you can't scrape it out with a stick.

It's clear to me that the universe
is just a little bit askew
and the lottery winnings meant for me
just happened to land on you.

I can't begin to tell you
how terrible it has been,
I'm under the weather and over the hill
and my candidate didn't get in.

I fear there may be more in store
I can't anticipate,
I'm out of control, I'm losing my grip,
I'm afraid I'm gaining weight.

I'm told that errors are not made
but I just can't agree,
this must be somebody else's karma,
it can't be coming to me.

I've been trying to convince the authorities
this is someone else's mess
and the perpetrator, who just skipped town,
gave them my name and address.

These are not my seeds that are ripening
or my lemons that are juiced,
these are somebody else's tough old chickens
that are coming home to roost.

I've been doing my doggone darndest
about cleaning up my act
and if I've been making any waves at all
they're just ripples and that's a fact.

I've been trying my best to abandon sloth
and open my eyes and awaken,
so this is someone else's very bad dream
or I'm totally mistaken.

And whoever's been spreading bad karma around,
I'd like to ask you whether
you couldn't please stop polluting the water,
'cause we all of us swim together.

I suffer your consequences,
so far as I'm concerned
whatever I do must rub off on you.
There's a lesson here to be learned

and we'd all of us have a better time
following the golden rule
if each and every one of us
stopped peeing in the pool.

LINDA STITT

REFUGE

I am prepared.
My cupboards are stocked and my freezer is full.
My sheets are clean and my toilet is disinfected.
I am prepared for uninvited guests
or unexpected company for dinner.
I have a three-month's supply of toilet paper.
    I am prepared for disaster.
My insurance policies are comprehensive,
if incomprehensible.
I have completed two duly witnessed powers of attorney.
My underwear is spotless
and there are two safety pins and a bandaid in my purse.
    I am prepared for poverty.
I have a list of friends and relatives
upon whom I could impose for a week's lodging
or at least a square meal.
    I am faultlessly prepared.
My travel reservations are made twelve weeks in advance
and I am at the airport four hours early.
My seat is selected and my meal is arranged.
    I am impeccably prepared.
The organizing that I had to do some day
was finished yesterday.
I have duplicates of my Daytimer and address book.
I have memorized my social insurance number
and photocopied my car ownership.
My wallet has a card with numbers to call
in case of emergency.
Some time in December
I enter all important dates on next year's calendar.
    I am prepared for death, —if not the moment thereafter.
My ledger is current and my bills are paid, some in advance.
My safety deposit box holds all the necessary papers,

My living will is in order
and my funeral arrangements are finalized.
I have signed the organ donor card on my driver's licence.
    I am meticulously prepared.
My snow tires were installed in September.
I have three spare heads for my electric toothbrush,
a drawer full of replacement fuses,
a dozen candles for when the lights go out
and several boxes of safety matches.
—You can never be too safe.
I have an extra pair of glasses
and a five-year subscription to *Prevention* magazine.
    I am prepared for the revolution.
My walls are braced, my windows barred, my door is reinforced.
There is a security guard at the front desk.
I wear my armour to bed and sleep lightly.
    I am prepared for tragedy.
I rehearse it daily
along with martyrdom and understated courage.
I am not prepared for mountains
or canyons
or prairie skies at cloudless midnights,
for the grandeur of a single anemone
or the challenge of spontaneity
or for the uncompromising honesty of poets and saints.
I am not prepared
for the winds that blow
through the barricade of my skin,
dredging up submerged fears,
excavating buried sorrows,
exposing truths
with no regard for shame or pride or sentiment,
carrying off all readiness,
cancelling all appointments,
dissolving all concealments,
revealing the magnificient insignificance
of all my preparations.

                  LINDA STITT

STORY

This is a poem, not a call to rebellion.
I tell you a story
from the dream files of my race.
The dream files are platelets of blood cells
whose inscription breathes
the secrets of the past before they have occurred.

Are you confused?
Good. That is what the government likes.
Here, then is the dream-story:
a young man in a government lab
washes dishes.
He does not know they contained
bio-chemical warfare.

One night, he breaks a dish.
He cuts his finger on the thin glass.
That night, this is what he dreams:
a pharaoh on a throne surveys
the blistered bodies
of his people, plague victims, dying all around.
The pharaoh tells loud stories
as a spell against the cursed plague.
The dreaming man sees two sides of his finger
close like the Red Sea, over the pharaoh and his people.

In a few months, the man feels ill.
His employer sends him on vacation, to Africa.
While there, he indulges himself
in the cheaply available bodies
of the natives.

He returns to work; his health fails.
His employer tells him he is dying

of a disease from Africa.
The man's disease thrashes across the planet
the same disease meant to ensure
the planet's safety for consumerism
now consumes its people.

Humans topple like the healthy cells
remaining in the man
and the government tells his story, loudly,
stopping as far back as Africa.

His own platelets implode;
they hold no strike against invasive authority.
His white blood cells
swim idly, perhaps watching t.v.
while infectious lies
seep across the man's body, the nation.

This last is a dream sequence
people toppling with lies
the government promoted.
It is a dream sequence from the files
of my race and this is a poem
and not a call to rebellion.

CHARLENE JONES

ADVICE TO WOMEN

Never make love with a poet,
    remember these words that I've said,
while you fuck with alacrity,
he'll be distractedly
making a poem in his head.
And the greatest delights of a poet,
    which he never can share with you,
are self-observation
and verbalization
and writing it down when he's through.

                              LINDA STITT

BODY WISDOM

The body knows
      breathing in
      breathing out
what the senses are about,
translating all impressions
into bright
      boiling bubbling
      rippling pulsing
      shuddering and shaking
tides of light,
incorporating each sensation into bliss.
The body
      breathing in
      breathing out
was made for this,
this clear instinctive awesome knowing
that is not bounded by the skin
and can perceive without, within
and everywhere,
ecstasy without identity,
the glory that the mind can not yet bear.

LINDA STITT

LOVE

Love calls you   now you are afraid
love does not come in colours you know
love does not speak softly
love has no voice but thunder and winds
and pulls your little world and pulls your little world
you tug back, you want shelter
love ignores this
love denies you comfort and sweet pretense
love welcomes chaos
as her politics are anarchy
love refuses what you know
pushes you for more you cannot refuse
its true you loved and loved and now love
wants more
love is within and this turns you
in your sleep in red-eyed dawn you weep
and wonder what sings and what is alone
is it love, is it love?
does it come knocking softly, does it wait
how can it be, this slashing at what you see
is this love, this question, this aching
this love punctures your confidence
shakes your complaisance
you quake at the root as you open the door.

CHARLENE JONES

LONG RANGE ROMANCE

I have learned, in my dotage,
whatever befall
I must love from a distance
or love not at all.

Better by furlongs
a trifle aloof,
a tittle afar
than under one roof.

Vastly preferred,
        as everyone knows,
to coming to grips
or coming to blows.

Not caught in the grasp
or caught in the act,
mileage maintains
illusion intact.

Passion is all
very well, in its place,
but give me an interval,
give me some space.

When next you're in town,
come by for a night
of amorous ecstasy,
bliss and delight,

of the damp spot that always
ends up underneath
my quivering haunches,
of hair in my teeth,

of a kitchen reduced
to a cluttered condition
and a toilet seat left
in the upright position.

Then leave in the morning,
while ardour still rages,
and go some place where
I won't see you for ages.

I'll love you much longer,
I'll love you much better
by e-mail or telephone,
postcard or letter.

I'll probably love you
all of my life
if you visit but rarely
and live with your wife.

LINDA STITT

USEFUL BOYS

Fran Leibowitz states in *Vanity Fair*
we have no more use for boys -
testosterone has outlived its usefulness
hard muscles as good as toys

She says we'll have no more real wars
for which I'm grateful, it's true
but on the point of no use for boys,
honey, have I got a use for you!

I can use you in the morning
to bring my morning tea.
You can sit beside my bed
or sit upon my knee
Fran Leibowitz thinks you're outdated, it's true
but honey, I've got a use for you.

You can mow my back lawn,
you can plough a field for me.
You can sprinkle seeds in my new earth
in whatever loose earth you see
Fran Leibowitz believes you're finished, it's true
but sugar, have I got a use for you.

Time was I, too, thought boys extraneous
too loud, a little fearsome and too adventurous.
Since then I've discovered boys become men
and their formerly annoying habits are more than compensated for
by the amazing capacity to fill, thrust, jiggle, bounce
push and compel me into a state of joyful oblivion.

Fran Liebowitz you may be smart it's true
but honey, have I got some news for you.

CHARLENE JONES

BLISS PIG

I am a bliss pig,
rooting in the moment
to find the rapture
buried in the mundane.
I have a nose for delight,
a feline organ
which tastes the odours of the present,
feasting on the ordinary.
Every blossoming instant
impregnated with awareness
bears the fruit of the divine.
    I will find it.
    I will crunch the bitter bones of now
    and savour their secret centre.
    I will gnaw through the husk of despair
    and sip the nectar
    at the heart of the immediate.
        No ambrosia is safe from me.
        Hidden in anger,
        concealed in pain,
        cached beneath the gravestone of regret,
        I will discover it,
        turning the earth of each emotion
        to the light,
        gobbling the energy
        transformed to ecstasy.

LINDA STITT

PIG DREAMS

The pig never suspects herself
wrapped in tender plastic,
frozen, thawing under hot water
thinned to mere centimeters
of mostly flab and some of its meat.
No, in her best stall moments,
leaned up against the safe grey boards,
scratching her back with diligent satisfaction
and what would be in a more encouraged beast
delight, the pig has in her mind
a moment in spring
the smell of mown grass
streaking up her nostrils like a naked vision
the farmer opening the stall door
into a pillar of light
and blinking, the pig herself staggering
in the sun toward the trough.
Her snout quivers at the cool delicious water,
and just as she sees her wavering reflection
she snorts a loud obeisance
to the Goddess
whom she knows
she one day will be.

CHARLENE JONES

THE MAN IN BLACK

And I in my joy can wait for my hero,
wait for the man in black.
He's large, he's steady, I hope he's not bringing
the clowns and the angels all back.

I have sung by the well, by the tree in moonlight
have sung with a whisper of leaves
and even the night's crushing velvet has heard me
describe my false hopes and my pleas,

That he enter the gate in the thorn crowded hedge
that he glide past the slumbering slaves
his feet on the stairs sends to shiver my skin;
my past has all fled to its grave.

And it's you in my joy I have waited for,
the man in black it is you.
Your hands hold the moon on a sun disc of gold
that is just large enough for two.

CHARLENE JONES

COME AS YOU ARE or BEAUTY OF THE BEAST

My lover never came,
        I waited for him day and night
until I cracked my shell
and he stepped out into the light
        saying
                dry and tattered, worn and used,
                flawed though you be, old girl,
                you cannot be refused.
                The coin you offer will not be denied,
                blemished and dull, it has its other side
                and all is worthy, bright and clear,
                in this consummate moment
                my beloved
                now and here.

                      LINDA STITT

HOW WAS IT FOR YOU, BABY?

For me, it wasn't very much,
a rediscovering of touch;
electric tremors up my spine
and, in the darkness, inner shine
of liquids luminous and warm;
a redesigning of my form,
melting and reshaping to
accommodate itself to you;
sinuous, sensuous skin to clasp
spasmodically, a moan, a gasp,
a sun gone nova. Nothing new.
How was it, my beloved, for you?

LINDA STITT

AND IF YOU DON'T CALL

And if you don't call
that means the kingdom's lost
that means the weather's nasty
that means the game's been tossed

that means it was a dialogue
between you and your pride
one of you was quick to win
the other of you lied

that means my face is slipping
and the red heat light is on
the whole event was just one night
the whole event is gone

that means you've found another
and she's good in your skin
she knows to bring the music
when her wisdom's running thin

ah, there's nothing much I brought you
from the daylight or the past
maybe a sliver of the light
but nothing that would last.

CHARLENE JONES

FAST LOVE

What with hookers and healers
clairvoyants and dealers
I'm in love with ya honey
but I can't find my face

We got twenty minute yoga
where they hurry up to slow ya
sixty second shiatsu
you wanna know if I love you?

What with thinkers and feelers
and cyberspace stealers
I love you baby
but the whole place is mad

we got a lawyer, a masseuse
macromicro and guava juice
being in love is no use
the whole place is a mess

what with internet, websites
I'm on chat lines all night
too busy to hit the avenue
you wanna know if I love you?

it's all multi and global
environmental is noble
I don't forget the ozone
just can't find my way home

you're a face and I know you
like the photo I showed you
someone looked a lot like me
but I love you, don't you see?

all the new age teachers
and the television preachers
telling us the way it has to be
everybody selling something
even if they give it to you free.

CHARLENE JONES

CRYING SHAME

I once had a very nice gentleman friend
who thought the world of me,
that everything about me
was just as it should be.
He liked my sense of humour,
my values and my friends.
He liked my aspirations,
he liked my means and ends.
He thought he knew my secrets,
he liked the books I read,
he voiced his warm approval
of everything I said.
    But all the time he thought he knew me,
      I saw that he could not see through me.
          He did not see my cowardice, my anger, or my greed,
          my lazy love of leisure, my inadequacy's need.
He thought that I was not too short,
too frantic or too fat.
So I just up and left him flat.
    How do you trust a man like that?

LINDA STITT

THE TENTH MOUNTAIN

Being with you reminds me of failure
the scattering flowers dying at our feet
our urgent need to say
the one thing we cannot say

Being with you I tolerate
the holes in life
because I see so clearly in me
the holes I hate

Being with you I am brought down
before the mirror. I see the flesh
its age and decay and impossible!
the same for you

Being with you moves me to the tenth mountain
where frustration begins it's jagged walk back
I am irritated by my blood
its stupid mute pounding
and the curiously clear sign of what I lack

Being with you I hear the strongest silence
refusing to mend itself with words
and the ugly repetition of my breathing
against the squawk of night time birds

Being with you the whole world
displays its flaws and facades
and through the cracks in its painful truth
I see the light of God.

CHARLENE JONES

KISS

Whose lips kissed yours last night?
Not mine.
Mine grow chapped when wind
bangs at them, grow rough
in the heat of the sun.
Whose lips suckled amber,
suckled honey,
whose lips caught the day shadows
argued them away with touch
the brushing, slightly pulsing
touch those lips received, gave
whose lips?
                    Those lips crave
more today.

CHARLENE JONES

LOVE POEM

      There is nothing I can tell you
that you do not know.
I can just remind you
of what you are pretending you've forgotten
as you go
playing the game of hide and seek,
paying no mind
to the mind that thinks in waves of grace,
where what you seek you find.
      So find yourself,
unique and chosen over all,
in all, by all
to celebrate creation
in your own way,
on your own path,
with your own life as celebration.
      You need not worship
at somebody else's church,
pray to somebody's god,
sacrifice at someone's shrine.
You are the very essence of divine.
      So now remember,
now that our minds have met,
and keep it in mind to remind me
if I forget.

LINDA STITT

MIDNIGHT WOMAN

It isn't me he wants,
the long haired woman of his dreams.
She knows his every heart beat;
she seals his aching seams.

And when her lust is over
she lies beside him still
and calls him gentle lover
and gives to him her will.

She has no life but him
at noon or near midnight.
She walks into his darkness
and shows the path to light.

And if his mind should stray
to a narrow corridor,
she rejects him coldly
her boot heel on his core.

He cries out in anguish
release me from your pain.
He thinks it's me at times like these
though I tell him once again,

I'm not the demon temptress
though I really wish I could
I'm not your Lady Midnight;
I've never been that good.

I don't soothe your every sorrow.
I can't bend to each desire.
I don't hitch my heartbeat to yours
or lick my flames at your fire.

It's not me who's rejected you
not me who's hurt you so.
I'm not as tall as Midnight,
I'm not her, you know.

He hugs himself in comfort.
He says, you've hurt me so
There is no Lady Midnight
You did this, I know.

But I can see her dancing
her shadow on the wall
her long dark hair in halo
her flames are leaping tall.

And I can hear her chanting
though he covers up his ears
I'm your Lady Midnight—
deny me if you dare!

I own you in the morning,
when your youth could burst in lust
and I'll own you at your graveside
and all between is dust.

If you refuse to know me
and think I'm only real
I'll make you suffer, trust me
I'll crush you with my heel.

He did not hear her curses
as she knelt behind his ear.
It's you, he pointed to me
You're the only person here.

I left him in his crouching
I left him to his fate—
the one he was rejecting
was his own Eternal mate.

CHARLENE JONES

PRISON SHIP

The deck is cracking,
splintering beneath my feet
and, in the tides of this corrosive sea,
the keel is crumbling
with fatigue and rust.
I have been chained to these oars for eons.
Manacles are all I trust,
shackles and bars
and the protective shell that shelters me
from the terrible infinitude of heaven,
the awesome winds of change
and the icy indifference of the stars.
I have kept faith with slavery
and taken comfort in the certainty
of matters known and charted
but currents here are unfamiliar,
strange and threatening.
I grow faint hearted.
The captain is abandoning the wheel
and, left directionless, I do not know
what I should do or think or feel.
I am floundering on freedom.
Throw me a raft of concepts,
a lifelime of identity
and buoy me with beliefs.
I am about to fall,
swooning with fear,
into the ocean of myself,
dissolving in the waters of the all.

LINDA STITT

FOR PETER—CIAO

You came to me like spring,
gently at first,
almost imperceptibly,
then in a warm rush
melting the crystals
at the centre of my waters,
cascading through my arteries and veins,
singing along my nerves and nadis,
curling a liquid longing up my spine,
awakening me to senses and to seasons.
Now I am resurrected.
I dress myself in the fluid kiss of silk
and bare myself to the winds
licking my limbs.
I am open to summer's sensual embrace
and the lingering encirclement of autumn.
Each thrust of beauty penetrates
where ice once armoured me
against nature's insistence.
I yield now to the heat
of my own essence.

The forever winter
which I though was upon me
will not come
as long as your fingertips
love my skin,
as long as your memory
floods my flesh,
as long as I do not forget
your promise of always.

LINDA STITT

MY SON

I suppose you could wait
for the dream of eagles
soaring between cloud shadows,
chasing across a land broken like tiles,
could wait to force a shape of solitude
outline of person
against the throngs.

You might wait, croached in the dark alley
rich with the yearnings of ancestors,
your head bumping
into the palms of ghosts.

If so, if you were this patient,
child of my ocean's shore,
if the suck and kiss of tides
rampant in your blood
did not twist you at the moon,

I could not recognize
that choice penumbra
around the baby, child, young man
describing in acute detail
that penubra shimmering now

as you spin yourself again
this time into manhood.

CHARLENE JONES

LEAVE TAKING

Soft night tumbles in the window
colder air falling upon the blanket of today's heat
and the radio emits gentle jazz
cooing sighs like a baby in sleep.

It is too snug here.
You about to fall upon the accident which is life
about to jet across the planet's girth
in search of some myth I misplaced
beside the pillow of your crib
myths of giants and evils, the good
and of course, beauty.

Your cells, the one success
of these loins blind, repetitive cycles,
your cells defy gravity
enter stratosphere
and read the airplane magazine
        drink too much for the altitude
Your body, (mine before) lands disoriented
on the foreign soil I walked long ago
welcome in the way of foreigners, softly
as though in landing
you bring a cold draft, an early night
on the full cotton batting of the day.

In the stretch of mind from here to there
my feet tap out an itchy gypsy rhythm,
impatient against the jazz,
my soul speaking tones of envy, and pride.
"Travel well, son."

CHARLENE JONES

go stupid

I go stupid like the corner whore on a cold night,
skirt a waistband and not enough boot;

I go stupid like the candy-apple suckin' 14 year old girl
scraped knees and dirty shirt
wants to give her small tits to the first boy who'll give her more.

I go stupid like the clogged drain
in a poor village in monsoon season,
all hair and stuck and glued with density.

I go stupid like the fat seer in the marketplace
when you've crossed her palm with silver
but your five bucks is used up.

I go stupid like the dumb-fuck love struck boy
first time ecstasy peels his nerves into heaven
standing on her stoop, leaning on the post,
leaving his eyes behind, on her, as a gift.

I go stupid as a car stalled in the middle of traffic.
I get out and kick my own tires.

I go stupid as the blank stare of dirty snow.
I go stupid as a fly against the window pane.

I go stupid without shoes
or dressed in raincoats
when the sun shines.

I go stupid as a broken tea bag,
empty gas tank, as one old shoe
on the busy highway.

I go stupid into the world
or somedays, I don't go at all.

    CHARLENE JONES

REGRETS

I am sorry
I am so damn sorry
that not all fairy tales
can come true,
that sometimes
happily ever after
only means for a year or two.

And I am sorry,
so very sorry
for the thoughtless things
I often do,
that all of my well meant
manipulations
don't turn out like I wanted them to.

I am sorry,
extremely sorry
for the sordid sins
of the human race,
we war and kill
and starve our children
and make a sorry mess of the place.

And I am sorry,
existentially sorry
at the lack of any
divine interventions
to punish evil
and set things right
and reward all those with good intentions.

I am happy,
mindlessly happy
when I give it all over
and don't give a damn
and change what I can
and forgive what I can't
and forget about how sorry I am.

                        LINDA STITT

THE LINE I FORGOT

I forgot this side of it, the heartburn, the vague headache. Here searching for an image or a word, the thought perhaps of feathers on a bed—that one taken from a young poet's tongue, lifted with silver tongs and my most polite smile. He couldn't refuse, his hands were cuffed in literary lace.

I can't tell, the sounds execute my thoughts, my jaw lies along the cradle of my skull like a mockery, mobile, floating, ineffectually forever opening and closing.
So this is the line I forgot, the one that refused to bring peace although I had sued and sued. There were no more places to put the words, there were no more frozen nights across Lake Ontario, or the spring run of smelt or the bushels of baby life, possibilities I had used them all in walking the boardwalk at midnight, someone else's midnight, returning to you endlessly in my mind.
I am circled in a lariat wide as my life, but still bound by the single point and still crazed by the thrust for freedom and the flight toward the center of your heart.

CHARLENE JONES

IN EXTREMIS

I weep to think of what we almost were,
of what we might have been,
for we have grown greedy and petty and mean
and aspire no higher
than sexual gratification
and a forty-five inch screen.
We have abandoned karma
for blind, capricious luck.
We are what we own,
how we dress
and who we fuck.

We pray to satisfy our senses;
lust is our only passion.
We have grown jaded
and degraded,
conforming to egregious,
decadent fashion.
Violence is no longer
something we recoil from and deplore,
suffering just whets our appetite for more,
carnage is a way of keeping score.

Our children are barbarians,
offspring of our indifference and neglect;
kindness, courtesy, respect
are weakness in their eyes.
We teach them how to trivialize
nobility.
We mock our elders
and we scorn the wise
and wealth,
though some may feign that they disdain it,

forgives whatever cruelties are done
in order to obtain it.
We sexualize our daughters,
nymphets all,
coarsen our sons
and give our issue
as wage slaves to the corporations.
Possessions are our obligations.
Our dreams are woven of such tainted tissue
that celebrity is our apotheosis.
We defile our wholeness
with religious, racial, national neurosis.
We have betrayed our birthright,
destined ourselves to die,
writhing, upon corrupted ground,
beside a clotted sea,
beneath a curdled sky.

And still,
should one brief moment of illumination
penetrate the nightmare realm
of our complacency,
we may yet find ourselves
sufficiently shaken
to open our delusion-shuttered eyes
and awaken.

LINDA STITT

DISCRIMINATION ASPIRATION

I will attempt to cope with fear
given this one condition;—
      somebody has to help me decide
      if it's paranoia
           or premonition.

                    LINDA STITT

IN THE BONE

I am indifferent to immortality.
Oblivion is immaterial to me.
Both evolution and extinction move to light
and I require no memory,
no dream of flesh
to tempt me into clinging yet again.

But today,
reading of the discovery
of a Neanderthal flute
      formed of a protohuman femur
      to voice the intrinsic diatonic scale,
I modify the all-consuming scope
of my proposed cremation.

Save back my long bone from the flame.
It is the instrument where music,
      bred in the marrow,
waits throughout millennia
and, while my song lies silent in potential,
I shall live as long as there is breath.

LINDA STITT

HERITAGE

It makes no sense to curse the blood,
the pot ought not decry the clay.
The faults that makes the vessel weak
will give it strength some other way.

The pain inherent in the flesh
will teach the spirit to endure
and the potential to pollute
can rouse and emphasize the pure.

What grand defilements lie in me
are, to the greater being, small
and, were this life not given me,
I should have had no life at all.

The sins to which I am the heir
could fetter me with resignation
but consciousness, dissolving bonds,
brings liberty and transmutation.

I bear my father in my bones;
I wear my mother on my face
and how I spend their legacy
is my own triumph or disgrace.

Examining by birthright,
I've reached this point of view,
>we all of us get whatever we get
>and do what we choose to do.

LINDA STITT

DAUGHTER'S POEM

The price you pay for having a mother
is bowing to the tyranny of the telephone.
You can't get up in the morning and say
I don't think I'll take any calls today,
not when you have a mother who lives alone.

The price you pay for having a mother
is usually consumerism's full, outlandish price.
You don't look for a bargain in something worn
or a little faded or frayed or torn
because it's for your mother and you want it really nice.

The price you pay for having a mother
is altering the way you'd normally behave
in the clinic, when you've waited for a long, long while
but you don't lose your patience and you keep your smile
because your mother's being patient and your mother's being brave.

The price you pay for having a mother
who is weak and dependent and sometimes a little vague
is dealing with a system you would otherwise avoid
and, for any help they give, you're grateful, even overjoyed.
For your mother you'd consort with the devil or the plague.

The price you pay for having a mother
is examining your values and the truths that you believe,
seeing angels coming forward from the ranks that you neglect,
finding strangers offering to help where you would least expect,
and a kindness to your mother is the greatest blessing that you could
receive.

The price you pay for having a mother
is keeping all your carpings to yourself, where they belong,
and checking your unwholesome and ill-tempered attitudes
and not indulging in your blue and black and stormy moods,
'cause she's your mother and she's always sure to know when something's wrong.

The price you pay for having a mother
is taking one day at a time, and then another and another
and planning little and staying on call
and doing it gladly for, after all,
it's a very small price to pay for having a mother.

LINDA STITT

ROSEMARY

The massive stone of her heart drops
one by one the pebbles of her future,
lightening today.
She has grey; grey clouds of hair
grey circles under her eyes
grey ashes in the layer just beneath skin
grey is hers.
Lavender blooms in her front yard,
under a layer of white snow
gathered at the edges
almost fluted by her shovel
like the border of pies she baked,
once, long ago, yesterday.

Her arm waves in the air, the wing of a solitary bird
reaching to slice the pie
but lands against the iron railing
of a hospital bed.
Her flight disturbs a machine
which bleats rhythmically in protest.

"Rosemary" the nurse's eyes peer
through a long fog at her
"Rosemary, you must not..."

Weigh the pulses of silence
their burden, against the laughter
of her son's, her daughter's, her grandson's

faces serious now, nudging each other
through the near dark
an eager flock of startled youth
dismayed at this intrusion
at the rattling bones in her throat.

She, however,
throws one even glance over her shoulder to them,
the final one of many crumbs.
She wriggles her fingers in her apron's empty pocket
and, task complete,
sinks her feet into the warm mud of spring.

CHARLENE JONES

MY MOTHER

My mother is a tree
within whose branches hide my shoes,
glasses, purse, earrings, keys
everything I misplace.
This must be true, otherwise
I would not yell "MAWWOM"
like she was doing it on purpose
when things go missing.

My mother is a bird
who flutters in the branches of the tree
revealing books, dollar bills, a sock,
the ticket I thought I'd lost.
This must be true
or else things would not appear
in her presence
whenever I yell "MAWWOM"
as though she's doing it on purpose.

My mother chocks back the ocean
holds it with her teeth, which clench,
so I, a mere teen, a young sapling,
will not drown when the tides of moon
or spring thaw of my blood
chase me to the shore's edge.

My mother is the embrace of wind
upon the whole planet, carrying seeds
of new life, of possibility
and scattering them like breadcrumbs.
This must be true

or else my heart in her arms
would not open,
revealing a tree and in its branches,
a bird, singing.

CHARLENE JONES

PAST DUE

I should have grieved her better
when she died
I was too brave.
I set my tears aside,
    (I did not even know I lied)
and tended to the thousand
passing little things
bereavement brings.
I bore the loss with fortitude,
not to defile her passing
with unseemly sadness,
    to show I knew she had transcended
    the cares and troubles of this world,
    the weight of its collective madness,
        to demonstrate my equanimity,
        my clear, untroubled mind.
And, for a while,
I thought acceptance
had triumphed over anguish,
but now,
from unacknowledged depths of loneliness,
I find
a sorrow too profound to be denied,
for all my shallow posturing and pride.
And, in that depth, I know,
before I can let go
of honest mourning,
I must pay the countless tears I owe.

Then, if ever,
    but surely not until,
tranquillity will bless me with a still
and quiet peace

and guilt and grief will cease.
She will have had of me her due.
And learning this, beloved,
I give a gift to you.
> You do not owe me courage
> when I die.
> Grieve if you will
> and cry when you must cry.

LINDA STITT

OLD GODS

Those are the gods
whose rage thundered through my mother
collapsing her hands
to the cuff and claw of prey birds.

Gods whose wisdom flailed
my early innocent flesh
whose memory cupped my skull
the giant claw, great hand
a puppeteer.

You ask of angels
and when they appear
dismiss them
for being only
on the inside of your skull.

See - those cracks in the clouds
trace the blood vessels,
those far nebula
your dendrites dancing with synapse.

And that small touch of lightning?
The old gods, roaring as they tumble.

CHARLENE JONES

WHEN I GO OUT OF HERE

When I go out of here
I want it to be on a clear July day
with the clouds doing their fly thing
and the sky a bucket of nowhere
splashed on an empty sea
and me, I want to be on a horse
that tang smell of sweat and animal
that feel of muscle smooth and warm
in the sun that stands in one place
and the shadows never move.

I want to start at a walk
that just so, just so with the horse
nickering, pulling at the reins
so my arms switch forward
and my legs tighten against
the belly of the beast
and the day eases by us
with Queen Anne's Lace
and purple clover, coneflower
and the evil grandfather, natural prairie sage.

The trees for my canopies
on the hoof hardened trail
and this horse takes the wind
up its widening nostrils
flickers its tail
and into a canter
on the dapple down lane we set
The horse and I, and a day
I never forget.

When I go, at that final second
I want to be flying

across that meadow to my left
alongside the river, with the horse
taking my heft like no weight at all
tail up and head erect
      the horse runs straight
to hell or wherever they'll have me
He gallops all the way, then stops on a dime
and I keep on flying, free of time.

CHARLENE JONES

DEATH WISH

Do not pollute my final breath
with whimpering and whining,
but say how sweet the lindens smell
and that the sun is shining.

Sing me a song of thankfulness
and, if you can't sing, hum
for what has been a wondrous life
and what is yet to come.

Tell me no forked, demonic tale
or any fearful story,
just give me leave to move, in love,
from beauty into glory.

LINDA STITT

DEPTH RECOLLECTION

In my dream
I watched a bed of tender shoots
pierce through the soil
and, in an instant,
rise
to leaf and bud and glorious flower.

And I awoke
      with joy for beauty recognized so swift in its arising,
      with sorrow for beauty realized so sudden in its passing.

And, as I held the dream,
there sprung, from my own matrix,
memory
that every bloom is rooted in totality
and, though it withers, droops and disappears,
      returns its essence to the universal source,
it bears back to the womb of all creation
the sustenance of the bliss of being.

All of experience is mingled at the font;
no blossom springs in isolation
but is confluent in its depth
with the bright, fundamental nature
of all that is made manifest.

Nothing is ever lost.
Death nurtures life
and, in the heart of each brief burst of glory,
I see the face of one I loved.

LINDA STITT

VOID ESSENCE

Feel how the Chinook
curls round the rabbit's burrow
on the west side of the hill,
as he wrinkles his nose
at the possibility of spring,
and listens to the earthworms
dancing underground
to the slow rhythm
of the planet's pulse.
Space is no barrier,
she said,
when there is only space.

I lifted a dubious shoulder,
shrugging off comprehension.

But this afternoon,
as I sat in silence,
I smelled the fragrance
of the emperor's favourite tea,
brewing in an ornate porcelain pot
on a lacquered table
in the palace of a dynasty
long forgotten
and I realized
that time, also,
is meaningless
in emptiness.

LINDA STITT

SPINDRIFT

Like sourceless waves
that go and come
within the timeless,
we are but heartbeats
of the drum
of eternity,
fragile and ephemeral,
shaped by the hand
of beauty.

Abandon any hope
of permanence.
There is nothing here
to be maintained,
nothing to be guarded,
nothing restrained,
merely the endless,
formless flow
of all we think.
Till all we think we know
dissolves in glory
in the boundless waters of divinity,
to arch in rainbows
above the cascade of infinity.

LINDA STITT

OLD AGE SECURITY

I am an old lady
with ribbon braided in my hair,
I celebrate the matriarch, the crone.
My heart is naked
and my soul is bare
and I live for love alone,
for there is nothing else
when all is emanation of the One,
endlessly manifest
in infinite complexity.

Craving ceasing,
       almost done,
almost
I am a wise old woman,
       learning not to covet
       or to cling.
I wear ribbons in my hair
and I have everything.

                  LINDA STITT

OFF DUTY BUT IN SERVICE

…so many people i have been
in the costume of my skin
in the drama of my life
learner lover lovelorn wife
intellect imagination
wild emotion pure sensation
spendthrift chatelaine and hoarder
and in no sequential order
housemaid hippie debutante
someone's mother someone's aunt
someone's teacher someone's student
overzealous over prudent
audience and prima donna
flora floradora fauna
meat and bones and painted skin
heart on sleeve and hell within
mad one moment or perplexed
grasping greedily the next
taking definition from
all arisings as they come
sculpting me while i do live them
from the very names i give them
child and priestess empress crone
one of three two one alone
softly pillowy or bolstery
part of the upholstery
part of music part of cloud
wispy silent thunder loud
pulse vibration sound and fury
terrorizing judge and jury
rigged inculpable defendant
glory manifest resplendent
universe alive revolving
widdershins decay dissolving
bitterly congealing sweetly

i thought i knew myself completely
but all the selves i thought i knew
were passing by or passing through
passing fancies plain to say
here tomorrow gone today
the ephemera i find
in my mirror and my mind

and now as alterations swirl and spin
around my wondering within
reconstituting flesh with latter-
day accumulated matter
growing conscious plant and granite
spirit humankind and planet
changed in time and not in essence
everlasting adolescence
born in every moment dying
never fear and no denying
vegetating petrifying
hatching fledging falling flying...

LINDA STITT

MUSIC TEACHER

You don't need to think and you don't need to plan,
only relinquish fear,
your body knows the way to go to harmony,
it can do it right how, right here.
Don't be afraid of getting it wrong,
but try to stay aware,
you can see the dance that shapes your days
and know it's always there.
You just need to learn to look she said,
and she taught me the means to employ
and the winds came humming through my bones, flesh, skin,
and my belly sang Joy, Joy, Joy.
I heard the curling waves of bliss
that are the body's song
and left on its own, like a little lamb,
the mind just followed along.

LINDA STITT

POLISHING MY FOOTWORK

Recognizing the oneness,
the unity of being,
I shall harbour no ill will.

I will have no enemies,
no disgruntled relatives
or disappointed suitors
or drivers who cut me off in traffic.
Not dog owners who don't scoop
or cyclists who terrorize the sidewalks
or politicians who exempt themselves from precepts.
Not surly waiters
or apathetic sales clerks
or well-meaning but misguided gentlemen
who bring to crowded elevators
the reek of a magnum of aftershave.
Not the incompetent, the indifferent, the inane.

I will cultivate compassion
to temper my righteous indignation,
acknowledging my participation
in even the clumsiest steps
of the dance.

LINDA STITT

BORN AGAIN...AND AGAIN...

All is impermanent, the sages say;
all that is formed will surely pass away.
And, though experience has shown this to be so,
my little self refuses to let go,
holding to form, to concept and to dream
and all the many fleeting things I deem
essential parts of the essential me.
And when that turning comes where I could be
freed from delusion, from desire and hate
which bind me to the endless wheel of fate
I fear the ego, frantic to grasp afresh,
will flee to a waiting womb and gather flesh.

LINDA STITT

VEHICLE INSPECTION

I'm not doing badly
      for my age,
in fact,
      I'm pretty damn good.
The body's getting rusty
but I'm dandy under the hood.

LINDA STITT

APPROACHING MY 67TH BIRTHDAY

In awe of myself,
I watch and I wonder.

I soar and I dive.

I stumble and giggle and strive.

I travel and never arrive.

I thrive.

Older than I ever thought I'd get
and it's great to be alive.

                    LINDA STITT

ABOUT THE AUTHORS

LINDA STITT

Born in Huntsville, Ontario, and educated in Georgetown and Toronto, Linda lived for many years in Thunder Bay where she began the exploration of her evolution. As a result, she has become an active participant, rather than an impotent bystander, to the process which Carl Sagan describes as "matter coming to consciousness." She has two children who are almost as old as she is.

Linda returned to Toronto in 1978, working in a series of odd jobs until forced by friends to come out of the closet with her poetry in 1982. She became a member of the League of Canadian Poets in 1994. Now impossible to repress, Linda loves to give readings anywhere, anytime. As a member of Uncritical Mass, an ebullient trio of poets, she does so with gratifying frequency.

Her first book *Reflections From a Dusty Mirror* was published in February, 1983. Once enough copies of it were sold to make room in her closet, she proceeded with indecorous haste to produce her second collection, *What Do You Feed a Unicorn? Yesterday's Poetry* was released in September of 1984 and *It Was True at The Time* appeared in October, 1988. *Insights and Outlooks*, was published in November, 1991. Uncritical Mass in Consort, a collaboration of love, was launched in 1995 and *Adjust Your Set* was published in 1997.

CHARLENE DIANNE JONES

Charlene Dianne Jones was born in Toronto. She has travelled raucously and earnestly seeking something which may not exist. Charlene persists in this folly, even after leaving Boise State University with a double MA in Education and English.

She has been published in several Canadian and US journals including *Atlantis* and *Prairie Schooner*. Charlene is an astrologer, is involved in dreamwork and is an ordained Buddhist. Currently Charlene works as a pycho-spiritual guide. This is the second volume of poetry she has had published within the umbrella of Uncritical Mass.